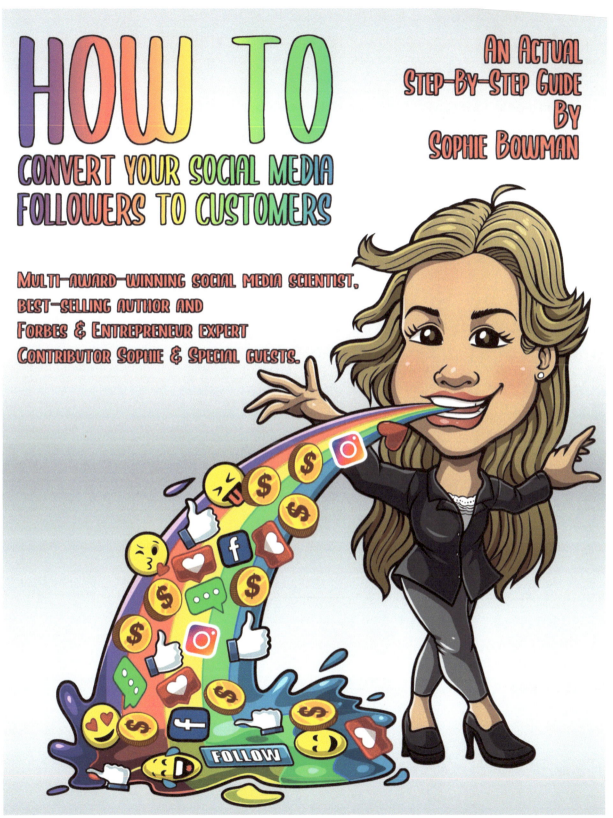

COPYRIGHT © 2022 BY SOPHIE BOWMAN

All rights reserved. Published 2022

Published by Don't Read In The Dark Publishing |

For information about special discounts for bulk purchases, please contact Don't Read in The Dark

All rights reserved. Library of Congress Cataloging-in-Publication Data. No part of this book may be reproduced, stored in a retrieval system, or transmitted, in any form or by any means, electronic or mechanical, including photocopying and recording without prior written permission from the publisher.

Sophie Bowman

First Edition Print

ISBN: 978-1-939670-55-7

Printed in the USA.

Although the author has made every effort to ensure that the information in this book was correct at press time, the author does not assume and hereby disclaims any liability to any party for any loss, damage, or disruption caused by errors or omissions, whether such errors or omissions result from negligence, accident, or any other cause. This is not financial or investment advice, while I might be a business consultant, I am not your business consultants.

Table of Contents

How to Convert Your Social Media Followers to Customers

4.	Introduction
6.	Why, though?
7.	BALMAIN Case Study
8.	Before You Launch the Giveaway
9.	Step 1
10.	The Hook...Here Fishy, Fishy!
11.	What to do Just Before You Launch the Giveaway
12.	A Little Help?
13.	The Giveaway Post
14.	Because Visuals Make Learning More Interesting…
15.	Promote the Post
16-18	Social Media Stata
19.	The Email Campaign
20.	Email Marketing Examples
21.	The Special Guests
22-24	The Quantum Plane: Tips to Increase Your Engagement on Instagram
25	Case Study: MarQuan x Sophie
26-27	Niki Peacock: Tips from the Influencer Realm
28-33	Junior Anthony: Converting Through Relationship-Building and Leveraging Your Own Ambassador's Followers
34	Eleonor Amora: Be Unapologetically Yourself to Make Your Fans Characters in Your Story
35	Note from the Author

WHO IS THAT BRIT?

Sophie is a Forbes and Entrepreneur.com published expert contributor in all things branding, digital marketing, social media, and business. Additionally, Sophie is a best-selling author and multi-award-winning entrepreneur. Hailing from London, Sophie launched her first creative agency online a decade ago so that she could travel the world and work from anywhere without pants.

Following an award-winning career in Public Relations and Digital Marketing, Sophie has worked on some serious campaigns including launch parties and events for John Legend, Kanye West, and Jamie Foxx. Sophie was part of the team behind London's infamous Notting Hill Carnival and the 2012 Olympics, as well as the release of DJ Khaled's last album, *Father of Asahd*, and Fat Joe's Hurricane Relief efforts for Puerto Rico.

In classic Sophie style, she was never going to have to wait on anyone for anything, so she challenged the status quo (as always) and educated herself in multiple industries including editorial, magazine sales, inbound marketing, PR, advertising, social media, and many more leading to the creation of the digital marketing assassin she is today.

Most recently, Sophie appeared on The Simonetta Lein TV Show Shark Tank Edition alongside Shark Tank's original OG, Kevin Harrington, and became the first-ever bikini model to sell signed limited edition NF art via Nora Coin.

Keep an eye out for her upcoming, patented technology swimwear and lingerie line in collaboration with some special guests.

After breaking her jaw in an accident two years ago and being on a liquid diet for two months (fun), Sophie lost weight, got scouted, and contracted to walk the runways of Miami Swim Week. Sophie currently holds the title Miss Bikini Fitness UK 2021.

Photo by @barryfreemanphotography

You can find her reading a book on a hidden beach somewhere in Mexico while plotting her next move.

To be continued…

1.
WHY, THOUGH?

Social media followers are cool and all, but if you're not converting them, they're simply voyeurs of your story, watching you from behind their iPhone screens giving you the occasional like or comment. While the latter two are important metrics, they are not the metrics you want to focus on.

What should I be focusing on? I hear you ask... conversion, conversion, CONVERSION!

Imagine if TikTok had been banned in 2020? Or Instagram? All those followers, likes, comments would be lost forever. All those dollars you invested in ads, POOF, gone. If you don't want to get caught with your proverbial pants down, you need to implement a simple strategy to start converting your fans to sales.

In Layman's Terms, social media followers are hot leads (they follow you, meaning they already show an interest in your brand). So, if you're not converting them, you're LITERALLY missing out on sales that are sitting there idle, ready for the taking.

Do I have your attention now? Good, let's begin.

2.
BALMAIN CASE STUDY

As the Social Media Director for a billionaire eCommerce entrepreneur, I was gifted a beautiful BALMAIN handbag for a giveaway to trial my conversion process.

The Results?

950 new email subscribers within 24 hours.
1K+ new followers
I retargeted the subscribers via email marketing 2 weeks later. Sales of the entrepreneur's makeup brand were up by over 38% at the end of that month. BOOM!

If you're a nerd like me, you just did the math on that to figure out what a 38% increase would mean for your sales. Nice, huh?

3.
BEFORE YOU LAUNCH THE GIVEAWAY

In the interests of catering to all readers, I'm assuming you may not have a CMS already (that's basically a platform allowing you to create an email template, send it to your entire email database at the same time, and track results, Grandma).

More advanced platforms are intelligent and will allow you to automate everything amongst other benefits. Think Fashion Nova and their 'You left this in your cart & it's selling out fast' style emails).

I personally prefer using MailChimp as I find it way more user-friendly, and it's easy to find designers who can customize MailChimp's templates with your branding.

1. Create a free account

2. Upload your email database (don't worry if you don't have any email subscribers yet, you soon will).

3. Customize an email template with your branding (or find someone to do this for you on Fiverr). You want it to look eye-pleasing so that people read it).

4. Ensure your MailChimp account is correctly linked to your email subscription (Again, Fiverr! - I could never figure out this Fiddly-F bag either.)

4.
STEP 1

Activate a popup box on your website that allows you to collect emails from site visitors. (If you're not sure how, Fiverr is your new BFF).

NOTE: Play around and try to learn how to customize your site yourself - it will save you time and money.

5.
THE HOOK... HERE FISHY, FISHY!

Unless a site visitor is a die-hard fan or a 'hater' (your new partner's ex or an unfriended friend, usually) who wants to track every move you make, no one is going to give you their email address unless you give them a reason to AKA The Hook (CTA).

Your hook can be anything from a 24-hour flash offer to a discount on first purchase, a gift with their first purchase, a giveaway, a free eBook download relevant to your industry, or access to a free member-only Facebook group. I prefer the giveaway, as the citizens of social media love free stuff.

6.
STEP 2

Customize the pop-up box with your giveaway image and brand tone text.

7.
WHAT TO DO JUST BEFORE YOU LAUNCH A GIVEAWAY

Here's the most important part of the giveaway matrix to drive traffic to your website, therefore gain more email subscribers. Are you sitting comfortably? Let's gooooo!

1. Create a free account on Bit.ly. Paste your link on the site to create a Bit.ly link of the blog page or landing page on your site giving more info about the giveaway. TIP: If you have neither, set the popup box to permanent and use your website homepage link to convert to a Bit.ly. Why? You can track where the most traffic comes from via your free Bit.ly account i.e., whether it's coming from your social media channels, your email marketing efforts, organic search, etc. so that you know where to invest most of your time or funds in your future campaigns.

2. Before you post your giveaway image on your social media channels, make sure you update your profile website links to your Bit.ly link.

3. Create a brand-specific hashtag for your giveaway so that you can track user-generated posts, especially if you're asking people to repost. Example #(your brand name)giveaway

8.
A LITTLE HELP?

Update your website link on all social media channels to your Bit.ly link.

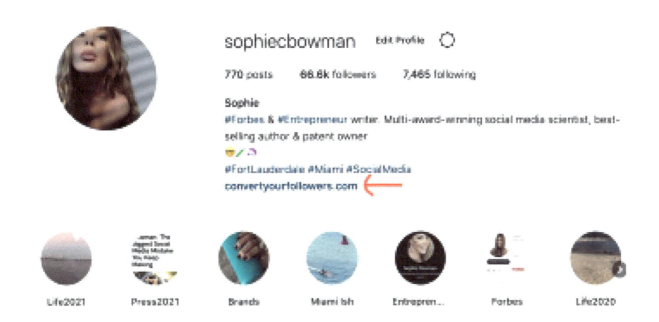

9.
THE GIVEAWAY POST

When you write your giveaway caption, make it easy for people to enter your giveaway via 'Link in Bio' OR ask them to tag 3 friends, repost, and add the blood of a virgin to enter via Instagram. This method brings out the worst in all of us because we all really are that lazy...

Always add the deadline for entries at the end of the caption, and when/how the winner will be announced to avoid triggering the contest-savvy keyboard warriors of social media. If you truly want to cover yourself from said people, draw up Terms & Conditions for the contest. Tedious, I know. But we live in a world infested with lazy people just watching and waiting for people to try and sue.

Within 24 hours of the contest deadline, congratulate the winner via Direct Message or email with instructions on how to claim their prize, and post the winner on your Story.

Because visuals make learning more interesting...

How to enter:

Click the link in my bio & enter your email address.

OR

Enter via Instagram:
1. Follow   and
2. Like this post
3. Comment tagging 2 friends that would love this prize
4. Copy & paste this caption and repost image on your Instagram feed tagging using # so that we can see your entry (which must stay up for a minimum of 30 days).

Liked by albertoferrari and 6,795 others

10.
PROMOTE THE POST

Social media engagement is kind of emotionally all over the place. You can do a 24-hour giveaway to generate an impulse response from users, or you can run it for a week and track the success to see which day of the week got the most sign-ups. I prefer the second method because that way you're beta testing TF out of life.

As little as $5-$20 a day can really increase the reach of your ad, attracting new followers and email subscribers. Promote where your audience hangs out, or again, beta test the process for your industry.

If I must explain why promoting a giveaway ad is more successful than promoting a quote or your latest product image, I can't help you… JK. Obviously, more people will click an ad if there's the chance to win something than they would if you promote an image of your logo, product, or quote.

Because the aim of this book is to give you an actual step-by-step guide instead of the usual generic crap, which we can only identify after we purchase it, I've even added in some social media demographics. You're welcome.

11.
SOCIAL MEDIA STATS

Facebook

- Number of monthly active users: 2.7 billion
- User main age group: 25-34 (26.3%)
- Average time spent on app daily: 38 mins
- Gender: 44% female, 56% male

Instagram

- Number of monthly active users: 1 billion
- User main age group: 25-34 (33.1%)
- Average time spent on app daily: 29 minutes • Gender: 57% female, 43% male

Twitter

- Number of monthly active users: 187 million • User main age group: 30-49 (44%)
- Average time spent on app daily: 3.5 minutes • Gender: 32% female, 68% male

LinkedIn

- Number of monthly active users: 738 million • User main age group: 46-55
- Average time spent on app daily: 3.5 minutes • Gender: 49% female, 51% male

TikTok

- Number of monthly active users: <u>100 million</u> • User main age group: 18 - 24
- Average time spent on app daily: 45 minutes • Gender: 59% female, 41% male

Snapchat

- Number of monthly active users: 265<u> million</u> • User main age group: 18 - 34 (75%)
- Average time spent on app daily: 26 minutes • Gender: 58% female, 40% male

YouTube

- Number of monthly active users: 2 billion
- User main age group: 15 - 25
- Average time spent on app daily: 42 hours • Gender: 72% female, 72% male

Pinterest

- Number of monthly active users: 400 million • User main age group: 30-49
- Average time spent on app daily: 14 minutes • Gender: 78% female, 22% male

These stats are correct as of 11/2021*

12.
THE EMAIL CAMPAIGN

Aim to send your first email to your email database within 7-10 days of the contest. Remember, offer value. The best email marketing emails offer an industry tip relevant to your database, an exclusive offer, and a link or two to your latest blog post(s) with a clickbaitification (catchy) title and a short intro to motivate readers to click.

Ensure your subject line also grabs attention.
Although emojis in the subject grab attention, they are usually interpreted as spam by receivers and ignored.

Use lower case letters for your subject line to help break through the overactive spam filters.

Consider sending 1-2 emails to your database every month. Make sure the content offers educational copy, promotions, blog links to drive traffic to your site and news that your readers will be interested in i.e., new product launches, networking events, or industry news. Offer value!

I've added a couple of examples of email newsletters I love. The design, branding, offer; everything is on point!

NATURAL, PROVEN & LIFE-CHANGING

SERIOUS ABOUT SKINCARE:

SPOTLIGHT ON:

I'm so delighted to get the stamp of approval from the iconic Beauty Bible - I'm a huge fan of the blog, as well as beauty guru founders Jo Fairley and Sarah Stacey. Beauty Bible loves my Biotech Pressed Serum.

"Lovely to use, skin definitely more vibrant, smells nicely 'botanical' - and we really like how make-up glides on. In fact, we're hard-pressed to find anything not to love about this..." Read the full article here.

My apologies for this having been out of stock, but the good news is, it's back! Grab yours here.

PLEASE NOTE:

Our prices will be increasing from the 1st October on all Antonia Burrell Holistic Skincare products.

SPECIAL READER OFFER:

First 20 online orders today will receive a complimentary Pure Therapy Facial Oil Serum - a potent intelligent formula which penetrates skin and calms, purifies, heals, refines and regulates the natural balance of problem skin for a glowing flawless complexion. Shop Now.

THINGS I LOVE:

I LOVE this inspiring quote by Iman. Throughout the animal kingdom, we're naturally drawn to confidence because it exudes courage, positivity, strength, leadership, power and knowledge As a brand with a vision to inspire happiness via skin confidence, there is nothing more beautiful to me than someone who's comfortable and confident in their own skin. Discover more about how I'm inspiring happiness, self esteem and skin confidence through life changing products at my blog.

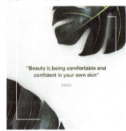

Be happy,
Love Antonia x

---

charlotte's book
skin   wellness   sex   aging

face

The skin issue that ages you more than wrinkles is...

[read now]

#ICYMI

The newest cellulite injection treatment really, really works. No joking around.

[read now]

get happy flora

The easiest way to get a healthy vagina is taking a special blend of probiotics and oregano oil.

[learn more]

🐥🐥🐥

Wishing you an amazing week. Stay raw. Have a question, comment, criticism, want me to cover something? Shoot me a note.

[email Robin]

Robin Levine (Ms. Shabin)

13.
THE SPECIAL GUESTS

Read on to discover top tips from the ultimate social media influencers. It's not about listening to celebrities and multi-million-follower influencers. Believe me, they do not manage their own social media growth, so I'll bet my butt they don't know their ass from their elbow when it comes to algorithms or game tactics. How do I know? Because I was paid to do it for them.

Follow the experts behind the scenes pulling the strings, not the puppets in the limelight.

14.
MARQUAN WILLIAMS

Bio: MarQuan Elijah Williams AKA Quantum Plane is the founder of Viral Influencer Promotions VIP / INFLEWNSE, a digital marketing agency specializing in providing Instagram growth to music artists and influencers. Hailing from Detroit, Quantum Plane is an established rap artist and social media superstar himself and is living proof that you can change your life. Just two years ago, he was living in a tent going days without food. He chose to fight back, turn his life around, follow his dreams, and travel as much as possible with this blessed work from anywhere lifestyle.

Tips to increase your Engagement on Instagram by The Quantum Plane

I get a lot of questions about this specific topic. Many people that see my Instagram account or profiles that I work with always ask me how to increase their interactions and engagement.

Here are a few tips that I've discovered work for me:

• Reels and videos seem to do better overall so keep that in mind when creating your content! Researching specific hashtags can be crucial. All you need is about "5-7" good tags to help the post gain more exposure. Just stay clear of banned hashtags. Spend a little extra time researching your hashtags to ensure you don't get shadowbanned for using an inappropriate tag.

• Check your insights for the best posting time based on the activity of your audience to help get more engagement.

• Join or build small engagement groups with others in your community and/or niche. This way every time one of you post you can just send it out to the group to get guaranteed interactions from other members.

• It's important to show love to others that you follow or within your groups, so when you post they will always return the same back to you.

• Replying to comments is very beneficial and many people forget the fact that each comment including your own replies counts towards your engagement rate. So, if you get 20 comments and respond to each one of them you will now have 40 comments.

• Emojis counts towards your comments also. Post-related comments and mentions will greatly benefit and your post.

• Increasing your engagement will help you land more brand deals and gain more authority on social media.

• If your engagement is already low avoid posting multiple times per day because you will eventually get people to unfollow you if you flood their timeline. Instead post multiple stories and limit your posting to no more than ONE POST A DAY.

• SHARE the post amongst your groups, to your story, and to friends/followers to get more traffic to your post.

• Cross-promote your Instagram page and post on other social media platforms to drive more traffic and engagement to your page.

• Post a story prior to your new post to alert your followers that you will be posting soon. If possible, add a countdown and stickers for more interactions.

• Write an appealing caption that will catch the reader's attention and focus on creating good quality content overall.

If you need more assistance or someone to handle your Instagram growth and engagement ongoing, feel free to contact @thequantumplane on IG.

15.
CASE STUDY
MarQuan x Sophie Bowman

Between juggling multiple business projects and walking Miami Swim Week, I stopped posting on Instagram for a long time, and my engagement dropped significantly.

MarQuan ran a trial on one of my Forbes posts a few days after my previous one crashed and burned (compared to my stats when I was previously active daily), and well, you can see the results for yourself below.

The best part? The comments are all relevant to the photo and real without any of those tell-tale spammy Bot comments.

BEFORE   AFTER

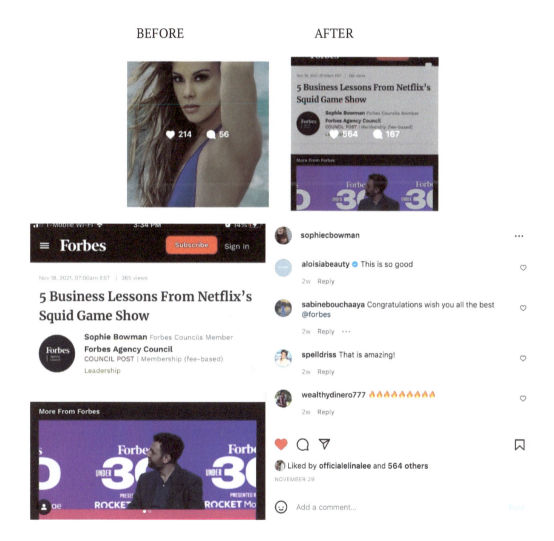

16.
NIKI PEACOCK

Bio: Hi, my name is Niki Peacock! I'm @Presidentniki on all platforms. I am one of the youngest curve up-and-coming social media content creators to reach a high level of success in just 2 years. I am 19 years old and have half a million on TikTok, 320k on Instagram, and many more platforms I roam in such as YouTube, Twitter, and Patreon. My specialty is promoting body confidence and inclusivity as well as the art of dance and being unapologetically yourself. I'm not afraid to be sexy and silly and that has led to a wide variety of success.

Tips from the Influencer Realm

Through Instagram, I get paid through live stream views. AKA I can go live as many times as I want if my entire account is advertisement friendly. Therefore, any content that I feel comfortable with doing that Instagram does not agree with (or find advertiser friendly) I have transferred to Patreon.

Keeping your public accounts advertiser-friendly helps insure brand deals and partnerships. So, if you want to delve deeper into your niche, I recommend creating a separate paid program where you can indulge your specialty. Through Patreon, I make about 10k a month in which I get to chat directly with my followers privately and in groups as well as promote new events I'm attending and upcoming posts and projects. The consumers feel like family, and they pay a monthly fee of your choosing to be a part of and support you. If you're good at something never, do it for free! A very special and unique thing to me is that I post Every. Single. Day, I think this is one of the most important things you can do online. People like people who they can rely on, you become their friend and someone they see and interact with every day, and let's face it in these times most of our friends are online.

Parasocial relationships run the internet especially on places like YouTube and Instagram where they see your face and actions along with words and shopping features. Every single platform I use has at least one post a day. Cross promoting is everything!!!!! I post on Instagram about Twitter, on Twitter about YouTube, on YouTube about Patreon, and so on and so forth. Each of the social media's you have has the chance to earn you Money and diversifying your portfolio guarantees you that if one profile isn't doing great or gets banned you have others to bounce back on.

One of my favorite things about social media is making connections! You have unlimited access to people of all job types, and you MUST reach out to them. Create a media kit and have your numbers and what makes you unique and how you stand out. Finding your niche is what's going to make you succeed. Coming from a gen z I am very fortunate to know what the young consumers want. We don't care about being perfect or fake we want REAL people with REAL accounts that will be honest with us and direct. If you are selling something you truly don't believe in, we won't believe in you either.

To make money and convert your followers to financial security you must take pride and joy in what you make. I love what I do and when I say Love that's an understatement. I enjoy chatting with my community and commenting and reading private messages it's what makes me happy and being able to make that a job is truly a blessing I will never take for granted. After all that I truly hope to create a relationship with You! Please follow my accounts down below and feel free to shoot me a message!

Instagram @presidentniki

YouTube presidentniki Niki peacock official channel

Twitter @presidentniki

Patreon @presidentniki

TikTok @presidentniki

Snapchat @presidentniki

Bitclout @presidentniki

17.
JUNIOR ANTHONY

Bio: Junior Anthony is the founder and CEO of LiveSotori, a dynamic platform of online entrepreneurs achieving financial freedom and creating abundance in all aspects of life.

He is a self-made multimillionaire that started with a single dollar to his name and an absolute will to succeed. Through his arduous journey in his early twenties and living through homelessness on the streets of New York City, Junior found his breakthrough and created massive wealth for himself.

"Figure It Out" is his motto, for as long as you have an end goal, a decisive mindset, and the persistence to get there, the "how" will reveal itself. He now has deep compassion to help others to do the same and be that person whom he wished would have given him a chance to succeed when he needed it most.

Converting Through Relationship-Building and Leveraging Your Own Ambassador's Followers

Who I am and where I came from?

Have you ever been homeless for over a year?

Have you taken a bath from the sink of a McDonald's?

Have you ever spent hours searching for sleeping locations?

Have you ever slept in the basement of a community college?

Abandoned houses?

Trains?

Cars?

Jail cells?...

Have you ever woken up with an extremely painful burning sensation in your extremities?

Buried under a thick blanket of snow?

Have you ever felt the burning cold of the New York City winter? Ever felt powerless?

Well, I have.

My name is Junior Anthony, and I will be sharing with you how, despite any adversity, you can still turn your following into cold hard cash. Look, I didn't always have it easy...

One particularly memorable cold day in New York a few years ago (when I was homeless), I turned my keys to start my car in an attempt to warm myself up and wipe the snow from the windshield. But my car wouldn't start. At that moment, I realized that I had left my phone charging all night and killed the car battery, leaving me stranded. By morning, I was buried a few feet deep, trapped, and the terrifying realization that I may actually freeze to death or die of hunger (whichever came first) was my reality.

Thankfully, I survived!

A year later, I found myself with just $10 to my name. The safe secure job that I thought I had, laid me off due to a minor injury. I was left stuck and depressed. My girlfriend at the time had just called me and said she wanted to go out to eat. I agreed but was thinking to myself, "With what money?"

Approximately an hour later, we found ourselves at the nearest Panera Bread, where I spent $9 out of the $10 on a Baja mac and cheese. I was down to $1 and my hope of being successful was slowly fading away. Once seated, I excused myself to make one phone call, one last roll of the dice in hopes that the universe would work in my favor before I ended it all.

A few months prior, I had attempted to become a digital marketer and had built relationships with business owners. Again, it was not always easy. While standing at the front door of Panera Bread on the phone with the business owner I had just dialed, near the end of our five-minute conversation, he stated, "How do I know I can trust you? How am I to know that once I give you this money you will not just run off?" My response, and my first real attempt at negotiation, was, "You can pay me half now and a half when I get the job done." There was a moment of silence, and I understood that if I broke the silence, I would be giving him the victory. After 30 seconds of silence that felt like an hour, he finally replied, "Okay, where do I send the money?" A short electronic transfer ensued, and my previous $1 balance now had a few hundred dollars. That was the beginning of my multi-million-dollar empire.

At that moment, I knew nothing about Facebook ads or generating results for my client. But I knew that if I had one shot, just one opportunity, I would make something happen.

And I did.

You see, the truth is, I'm not special. I was simply able to figure out my journey to take me from point A to point B, which generated a couple of million dollars in less than two years. I'll be sharing some discoveries I found during that journey which will help you convert your followers and build a strong following. Or of course, you can get more insight on exactly step-by-step how I made over 1 million dollars in 9 months by converting just a small group of followers in my upcoming book, "More Human."

When I started, I did not know anything about building a digital marketing business. However, I learned that having strong networking and relationship-building skills are essential if you do not want to be replaced by artificial intelligence. Don't believe me? Ask the guy that picks up the garbage at your home. Oh yeah… you can't, he was replaced by those new trucks that now only require a single passenger to operate a machine that picks up the garbage.

I've found that the best thing about these skills is that they can be applied to any business or personal situation. For example, I was able to build a brand-new digital business that consists of online entrepreneurs who simply follow my relationship-building knowledge to successfully earn money online without any prior digital experience. These skills are often overlooked due to their simple nature; however, what many people don't know is that they are a hidden treasure which can open many doors for you.

What is LiveSotori?

I realized very quickly upon venturing into the online world that not only is it a world full of possibilities, but after spending years of trial and error with client after client, I also realized how difficult it was to understand all the available information. So, with a new determination after seeing this huge problem within the industry, I DECIDED TO BE THE CHANGE.

During the global pandemic, out of a need to help people who were struggling to learn how to generate an income source from the internet, I began coaching students inside of LiveSotori. LiveSotori helps give entrepreneurs the confidence they need to get started online. Many people see results in a few weeks or even just a few days! Most people within our company can produce $1k days, sometimes $2k days, and even $3k days all while still being a beginner. I even had the pleasure to witness someone who didn't have the ability to copy and paste before coming to me, and she was even able to make her first income online!

This is the result of learning a combination of different skills that allow you to connect with people and create lasting relationships. The one similarity that these members share to generate such massive success will be covered more later in this chapter. But first, let me explain a little more about my company as we will be circling back around to the main point. If you missed it, I would suggest re-reading the entire chapter.

Within my journey, there were a series of things that I learned, and believing in my plan with absolute certainty before it even started was crucial for me when attaining success. I tell my students, "If you have a Plan B then you are planning to fail." Why? Because

if you don't have belief in your own abilities, then why even start? With anything that you do, have confidence in yourself to dive in and crush it! Always have that end goal in mind with a 'no matter what' mentality. No matter what happens, I will get it done.

I have seen people in my online family be able to accomplish so much once they were able to conquer their own fears and practice the skill of confidence. This is where I say, "It is not what you do, it's who you have to become," and you must become a completely different person.

LiveSotori's massive growth is most likely since Sotorians (we have a cool name for our ambassadors) are aware that to see growth in themselves and in their financial life, they must develop not only good habits but also practice being proficient at high-income skills.

I designed my program in a way that allows entrepreneurs to support each other in a positive environment where it makes you feel comfortable enough to practice these skills and become a better person with great morals and values. This kind of uplifting atmosphere creates the perfect soil to grow anything. I knew that if I were to build a community, I would build it so that everyone could work together on the same project, and one person's weakness can be remedied with another person's strength.

Herein lies the importance of networking. If you take the time to get to know people at a different level, you will have the ability to reach your goals at a faster pace. However, to network, you need to learn how to build a connection first. I've seen for myself with my own company how an entrepreneur can go from being an introvert to a person who has the skill to print money and, at the same time, not only grow their following but also turn their social media into a profit-making machine.

Now that you know the basics, I want you to keep something in mind. No matter what type of technical information I give you if you don't have the correct mindset, nothing that I tell you or show you will matter. So, make sure you have an open mind and a set belief when trying to grow your income. Trust me, it makes a difference.

Why relationship building is my go-to success method

I strongly believe that relationship building is now the number 1 skill going into the next decade. As you can see from my story of rags-to-riches, that crucial skill was all I had as my asset at a time when I was completely broke and homeless. I didn't have money, I didn't have connections, I didn't have any influence at the time. But I had the ability to understand and create an instant relationship with anyone I met. This is the vital key to attaining massive success that most people overlook since it is something internal. If you master this skill set, there is no limit to your success and income.

Giant companies like Amazon and Apple focus heavily on cultivating strong relationships with their customers to understand how to better serve them and deliver what the customers need or want.

You can only truly understand someone once you build a relationship with them. Two important things to utilize when building relationships are the ability to relate through empathy and a burning desire to help make a difference in someone's life. Empathy is being able to sense other people's emotions and being able to imagine what they are thinking and feeling to essentially walk in their shoes. You need to be more interested in others than yourself and have complete self-awareness, humility, and great listening skills to develop empathy. I always tell my students, "God gave us two ears and one mouth for a reason."

Truthfully, most of us don't have good listening habits. We tend to rush people through conversations, assume what they will say and finish their sentences, and focus only on what we want to say next, or even fake paying attention to them. Imagine how effective your communication would be if you truly listen to the other person with full attention and a genuine curiosity?

Building strong relationships is super important because customers will stay loyal to you and your mission if they see that you truly care about them and what they need. Through my experience, I learned that when I put the needs of the customers before mine, my customers make sure that I'm in business because they now rely on me as well. My success is crucial to them. "People don't care how much you know until they know how much you care." This burning desire to help others has transformed me into a Master of Communication because I know exactly what to say and how to say things that matter to the person with whom I'm communicating.

I leverage social media to be able to connect with people on a massive scale. But at the end of the day, my method boils down to those two things I mentioned earlier - empathy and a burning desire to help others. That is why my followers are very loyal to me. They understand how much I care about them and their success. Social media gives people the opportunity to be social and build relationships with thousands of

people at once.

The vision

The primary reason for my intense focus on LiveSotori is our mission. When I was homeless, I desperately wanted someone to guide me in the right direction, or at the very least tell me what I was doing wrong. I luckily received that blessing which then excited me to pay it forward. I want to be that guiding light for people. My focus and my goal with LiveSotori are to create 100 millionaires - people with different stories, different backgrounds, and different reasons why they need to succeed.

We all know that you are only as successful as the people with whom you surround yourself. With LiveSotori, I can provide a powerful environment for entrepreneurs to build long-lasting friendships, enhance their quality of life, and develop their talents. Think of it more like a new way of living.

In this Digital Age, it is important for you to stand out from the crowd, whether you are trying to grow your network or just trying to make a connection. The system already works. Now all you must do is rinse, repeat, and socialize.

Instagram: @junioranthonylive www.livesotori.com

18.
ELEONOR AMORA

Bio: Eleonor is the founder and CEO of the House of Sovereignty global enterprise and the Publishing House of Sovereignty. An internationally acclaimed energy healer, spiritual coach, and award-winning multiple best-selling author who founded the world's biggest spiritual multiplex enterprise. She teaches everyone how past pain can be turned into fierce inner strength.

Be Unapologetically Yourself to Make your Fans Characters in Your Story

Social media plays a pivotal role in all my business ventures and can be a major secret weapon when you know how to use it. My publishing house releases several co-authored books every year. I find a large group of soul sisters who put their heart and soul into words to create inspirational stories. On book launch day, all co-authors collectively use our own social media platforms to promote the book, pushing the books to become Amazon best-sellers across multiple countries.

I recently purchased one of the most successful magazines in my hometown, Sweden, for which I also use social media to drive traffic to the online magazine to increase our readership and raise awareness outside of Europe.

If you're planning to use social media to promote your products or services, share your brand story with your followers, unapologetically. For example, authors or publishers could post excerpts from their book, reviews of the book, and even ask followers which story idea they like from three different ideas. Engaging with your fans is everything; pull them into your story, so that they become part of it.

www.houseofsovereignty.com
Instagram: @eleonor_amora

19.
NOTE FROM THE AUTHOR

Dear Human reading this,

Thank you for your faith in me and trusting me to help guide you on your social media conversion journey. I love to see people winning. The fact I made a lot of enemies in the industry by sharing these insider secrets is of no concern to me. If you're not hated, you're doing something wrong, and you're not making enough noise in your field...

Sending a huge thank you to all my amazing special guest authors who took the time to share their wealth of knowledge on how they have grown, and continue to build, their social media presence. As a special gift, you're invited to join my Facebook group of like-minded entrepreneurs where you can network, brainstorm, and get quick responses and solutions to business questions and problems. Join me on my mission to create a business owner community where we use one another's' services to keep the money within our little online world and ensure our business owner community is thriving instead of surviving; we're all in this together!

Every guest author is legit, cool people. Don't be afraid to follow and reach out to them. Follow this guide step-by-step, and you will start seeing a shift in your social media success. You got this!

Until next time...

Sophie xoxo

Instagram: @sophiecbowman

Facebook Group: https://www.facebook.com/groups/socialmediaconversion/ www.convertyourfollowers.com

www.thesophiacollection.com

www.brandbrandingpr.com

www.giftsforentrepreneurs.com

CPSIA information can be obtained
at www.ICGtesting.com
Printed in the USA
BVHW021016210322
632004BV00002B/10